SECRETS OF THE JAPANESE ART OF WARFARE

An annotated translation of Yamamoto Kansuke's classic treatise on strategy and tactics

THOMAS CLEARY

TUTTLE Publishing

Tokyo | Rutland, Vermont | Singapore

The Tuttle Story: "Books to Span the East and West"

Most people are surprised to learn that the world's largest publisher of books on Asia had its humble beginnings in the tiny American state of Vermont. The company's founder, Charles E. Tuttle, belonged to a New England family steeped in publishing. And his first love was naturally books—especially old and rare editions.

Immediately after WW II, serving in Tokyo under General Douglas MacArthur, Tuttle was tasked with reviving the Japanese publishing industry. He later founded the Charles E. Tuttle Publishing Company, which thrives today as one of the world's leading independent publishers.

Though a westerner, Tuttle was hugely instrumental in bringing a knowledge of Japan and Asia to a world hungry for information about the East. By the time of his death in 1993, Tuttle had published over 6,000 books on Asian culture, history and art—a legacy honored by the Japanese emperor with the "Order of the Sacred Treasure," the highest tribute Japan can bestow upon a non-Japanese.

With a backlist of 1,500 titles, Tuttle Publishing is more active today than at any time in its past—inspired by Charles Tuttle's core mission to publish fine books to span the East and West and provide a greater understanding of each.

Published by Tuttle Publishing, an imprint of Periplus Editions (HK) Ltd.

www.tuttlepublishing.com

Copyright © 2012 Thomas Cleary

Library of Congress Cataloging-in-Publication Data

Cleary, Thomas F., 1949-
  Secrets of the Japanese art of warfare : from the school of certain victory / Thomas Cleary.
    p. cm.
  ISBN 978-4-8053-1220-9 (hardcover)
  1. Martial arts--Japan--History. I. Title.
  GV1100.77.A2C54 2012
  796.815--dc23

ISBN 978-4-8053-1220-9

First edition
16 15 14 13 12   6 5 4 3 2 1
1206RP

Printed in China

Distributed by

North America, Latin America & Europe
Tuttle Publishing
364 Innovation Drive
North Clarendon, VT 05759-9436 U.S.A.
Tel: 1 (802) 773-8930
Fax: 1 (802) 773-6993
info@tuttlepublishing.com
www.tuttlepublishing.com

Japan
Tuttle Publishing
Yaekari Building, 3rd Floor
5-4-12 Osaki
Shinagawa-ku
Tokyo 141 0032
Tel: (81) 3 5437-0171
Fax: (81) 3 5437-0755
sales@tuttle.co.jp
www.tuttle.co.jp

Asia Pacific
Berkeley Books Pte. Ltd.
61 Tai Seng Avenue #02-12
Singapore 534167
Tel: (65) 6280-1330
Fax: (65) 6280-6290
inquiries@periplus.com.sg
www.periplus.com

TUTTLE PUBLISHING' is a registered trademark of Tuttle Publishing, a division of Periplus Editions (HK) Ltd.

Contents

PART IV

The Pole

PART V

The Spear

PART VI

Archery

PART VII

Firearms

PART VIII

Human Advantages

PART IX

Advantages of Terrain

PART X

Advantages of the Sky

Translator's Introduction

*Secrets of the Japanese Art of Warfare** is attributed to the legendary Yamamoto Kansuke (1501–1561), whose name as a lay monk was Dōki, "Demon of the Way"—an outstanding soldier, commander, and strategist of Japan's *Sengoku jidai* or Era of Warring States. A mysterious man of humble origin, largely obscured by myth, Kansuke distinguished himself in the service of the redoubtable Takeda Shingen (1521–1573), heir to a long lineage of warriors and one of the most active and successful warlords of the time. The school of military science and martial arts that this text represents emphasizes a special style of strategy known as *the art of certain victory*.

This school subsequently produced some distinguished warriors and military scientists, notably the famous

---

* A more faithful translation of the title is *Secrets of the Arts of Warfare.*

swordsman Miyamoto Musashi. It was adopted by the deified Shogun Tokugawa Ieyasu, who ultimately pacified war-torn Japan in the early seventeenth century.

The origin of this school of invincibility is related in *Essentials of Military Matters* by Yamaga Takatsune, one of its heirs:

> The law of the warrior starts with rectitude and ends with victory. This basis is found in the deified ruler's establishment of law on the basis of warfare. Rectitude means staying on one line without deviation, victory means winning, not being overcome by others. It began with Yamamoto Haruyuki (Kansuke) as the teacher of military science who passed it on to Takeda Shingen of Kai province, determining Shingen's system of warfare. In his lifetime Shingen fought thirty-nine battles without a single defeat. This is a teaching of certain invincibility, a comprehensive tradition including defense, offense, siege, security, massive combat, minimal combat, mountains and rivers, sea and land, night combat, night security, ambush, and all other military matters, involving nothing risky at all.[*]

Kansuke himself is recorded in this very text as saying that there is no way to guarantee success, but the strategic corollary of this is to know when to act and when to refrain. It is for this reason that Yamaga refers to winning

---

[*]   Translated in *Samurai Wisdom: Lessons from Japan's Warrior Culture* by Thomas Cleary.

here as "not being overcome." In the experience of the professional warrior, this means living to fight another day. Yamaga's representation that this method involves no risk, seemingly absurd in the context of armed conflict, refers to the essential stance of this approach to warfare, that it is the art of the advantage, engaging only as and when it is advantageous. This is closely associated with the strategic principle of waiting for adversaries to make the first move, to avoid arbitrary exposure and remain unreadable, and to be able to take advantage of the form and momentum of the enemy.

The traditional portrait of Yamamoto Kansuke may be a reflection of the ambiguity in this posture of seeking certain victory in spite of the impossibility of assuring it. Reputedly a hideous man both despised and admired, rejected by the patron of his own teacher, Kansuke is pictured as already having lost the use of one eye, one hand, and one leg from wounds by the time he was appointed infantry commander and strategic consultant by the young warlord Takeda Shingen. Ultimately he died in combat, a soldier to the end, but not before he was at least sixty years old.

Kansuke's successor in this school of military science, a man named Hayakawa Yukitoyo, was allied with associates of Takeda Shingen and Tokugawa Ieyasu, the future Shogun. Before becoming Shogun, Tokugawa Ieyasu also employed an obscure uncle of Kansuke as a military advisor. Subsequently Hayakawa Yukitoyo's successor Obata Kagenori (1570–1644) became a direct vassal of the house of Tokugawa. Obata was one of the teachers of

Yamaga Sokō (1622–1685), who came to be called the founder of Bushidō. A prolific author like Obata, Yamaga also studied with his designated successor Hōjō Ujinaga (1609–1670). Hōjō Ujinaga, like Obata Kagenori a direct retainer of the Shogun, was a teacher of the redoubtable Miyamoto Musashi, whose *Book of Five Rings* is now one of the best known works of its kind.

Yamamoto Kansuke's work emerged from the midst of warfare and predates the elaboration of martial arts by urban samurai that was carried out during the lengthy period of domestic peace under the Tokugawa shoguns. While it is therefore comparatively basic besides being simply succinct, as the work of a professional soldier absorbed in the realities of combat it contains essential and irreducible elements of training and tactics.

The controlling concepts of this science will naturally be recognized by all persons experienced in military, law enforcement, or other emergency response professions, as well as by martial artists and athletes, who will understand how to adapt them to their particular needs. The science of strategy, particularly the study of configuration and momentum in dynamic relations, can also illuminate tactical ambivalence in political affairs, as well as cultural and ideological weapons typically employed in psychological warfare.

—Thomas Cleary

PART I

General Discussion

The Sources of the Arts of Warfare

As for the sources of the arts of warfare, in China they began from the Yellow Emperor, while in our country they began from the divine age. Coming to the human age, the numbers of weapons increased, and the information on them is diverse. Here, ever since my youth I have been devoted to this path. Considering the techniques for long and short weapons, which to use and which to omit, if any are omitted victory is uncertain. The reason for this is that the space between you and the opponent differs with the occasion. For a distant opponent you use bow and arrow and firearms; for an enemy at middle range you use spear and halberd; for an enemy close at hand you use swords. For grappling at even closer quarters, a dagger less than a foot long is good.

Notes

The Yellow Emperor, a Chinese culture hero, is associated
with various Taoist arts, including the arts of lovemak-
ing and life extension as well as the arts of dominion and
warfare. In a Taoist text called *The Master of the Hidden
Storehouse* it is written that the Yellow Emperor waged war
with fire and water, radical means of mass destruction;
and the cryptic strategic manual called *The Book of Hidden Correspondences* is traditionally attributed to the Yellow Emperor. In Japanese mythology, the prime archetype
of the warrior-leader is called the Divine Warrior with the
Precious Lance, but the ideological elevation of martial
culture was a comparatively late historical development.

Teachers of the Arts of Warfare

Teachers of the arts of warfare transmit the advantages of
considering how to win with bow, spear, halberd, sword,
dagger, and other instruments of killing, striking when you
should strike, and not striking when you should not strike.
If you lack training in even one weapon, you should not be
called "a teacher of martial arts;" how much more should
we be wary of calling someone who is trained in only one
weapon "a teacher of martial arts."

The reason for this is that one who uses only the bow
should be called an archer, one who uses only the spear
should be called a lancer, and one who uses only the sword
should be called a swordsman. Each one should be designated by the specific name.

Notes

Confucius placed great emphasis on correct usage of terms, implying a common consensus of social values and a coherent correspondence between names and realities, embodied in the adherence of individuals and organizations to their designated roles in the socio-political order. In the historical context in which Kansuke's military manual was composed—an internally divided Japan under the rule of competing warlords—a practical implication of this admonition about correct usage of names is that when a warlord wanted to solicit a teacher of martial arts, in order to save time and effort for all concerned it should be made clear at the outset that this does not mean a master of one or another individual weapon but a comprehensive expert. While terminological precision past a certain degree can become uselessly overwrought in theoretical contexts, or comparatively unimportant or superficial in casual contexts, Kansuke's particularity in regard to terminology is an example of the general principle of organization for efficiency underlying many aspects of military science as a matter of practical necessity, or necessary practicality.

The Order of Transmission of the Arts of Warfare

As to the order of transmission of the arts of warfare, first we teach fist technique, to master the workings of the four limbs, mind, and body. Next we transmit techniques of short weaponry; next, techniques of long weapons; and after that, techniques of projectile weaponry. Linking these in order, after transmitting designs of human advantage, situational advantage, and natural advantage, we transmit the principles of all things to assist application.

Notes
This curriculum generally parallels development of sophistication and skills in civil life as well, so it can be used effectively to refine everyday attention to qualities and dynamics of physical economy, necessary tools and skills, human interactions, spatial relations, form and momentum, and patterns of adaptation and improvisation.

The Systematization of the Arts of Warfare
Teaching the arts of warfare in a systematically organized way is like a spelling system; it can apply to all things, when used with consideration according to the time. These arts can't be used for anything without consideration, as it would be hard to win that way. It is for this reason that the organizing structures of martial artists past and present differ, and are not uniform. This is why consideration is necessary.

Notes
The system outlined in this manual focuses on definitions of basics, organizing them in order to make them readily available to the mind for strategic recombination according to conditions. According to Yamaga Takatsune's description of this system in *Essentials of Military Matters,* "The training does not involve a lot of talk, and the

basics are not that many."[*] The same author also describes
the course of instruction in these terms: "The Yamamoto
system first teaches principles, then teaches about castles, battle formations, preparations, and operations, and
finally teaches arts of war and certain victory. The traditional teaching methods are still taken for guides."[†]

Five Trainings in the Arts of Warfare

In the arts of warfare there are what are known as five train-
ings. These are training of the eyes, training of the ears,
training of the mind, training of the hands, and training of
the feet. With the eyes you see forms, with the ears you
hear sounds, with the mind you contrive plans, with the
hands and feet you make movements. These are the terms
of the general outline.

Notes

Training of the eyes includes attention to reading body
language and facial expressions as well as sizing up
spaces and evaluating environments. Training of the ears
includes interpreting voice modulation, judging wind, and
discriminating background sounds. Training of the hands
and feet includes coordination between them, and con-
comitant concerns of balance and recovery. Contriving
plans, in this context, is more than planning maneuvers
at headquarters, as Kansuke emphasizes ability to assess

---

[*]   Cleary, *Samurai Wisdom*, p. 205.
[†]   Ibid. p. 206.

situations and think on your feet in the midst of action. In a state of stillness, the mind is also used as an organ of perception, like the eye, but ordinarily in martial arts this faculty is maximally accessible only in individual duels, and is less available and less reliable in the energetic chaos of mass combat.

The Arts of Warfare and Three Destructions

In the arts of warfare, there are what we call three destructions. One is to attack the unruly to pacify them. Second is to attack the unjust to correct them. Third is to attack the rebellious to make them docile.

Notes

Grounds of justification for warfare are proposed in various military manuals. While these are given in varying degrees of particularity and reflect a range of political philosophies, there are typically some essential similarities among them, including sentiments eventually reflected in the codification of international laws of war. Those given by Kansuke here are comparatively common, stated with a starkness and simplicity that is typical of this work and invites further consideration. Depending on interpretation of intent, it might be possible to derive refinements or variants of these principles articulated with more particularity in other contexts.

The Chinese military classics were one of the main sources for Japanese samurai. *Master Wei Liao,* composed during China's turbulent Era of Warring States—a

time somewhat similar to that of Yamamoto Kansuke—
expresses comparatively exacting opinions on the ethics of
warfare, some of which have not been adopted as international legal standards until relatively recent times:

> In general, a military force is not to attack an inof-
> fensive city and does not kill innocent people. To kill
> people's fathers and brothers, to profit from people's
> money and goods, and to enslave people's sons and
> daughters are all robbery.
>
> Therefore the military is to execute the violent
> and unruly and to stop injustice. Where a military
> force attacks, the farmers don't leave their work in
> the fields, the merchants don't leave their shops, the
> officials don't leave their offices—since the target is
> only the top man, the soldiers do not have to bloody
> their blades for everyone to be won over.

Another Chinese military classic, *The Warrior Code of the
Charioteers,* gives specific instructions for the protection
of innocents, including their means of livelihood, and
treatment of the wounded:

> When you enter the territory of an offender, let
> there be no desecration of sacred shrines, no hunt-
> ing in the fields, no destruction of infrastructure, no
> burning residential areas, no deforestation, no con-
> fiscation of domestic animals, grains, or machinery.
> When you see the old and the young, escort them to

safety and do not let them get hurt; and even if you meet able-bodied men, do not attack them if they do not engage you in confrontation. If you wound opponents, give them medical treatment and send them home.[*]

In *The Education of Warriors*, the 17th century Japanese military scientist Yamaga Sokō (1622–1685), a recognized successor of the school of Yamamoto Kansuke, cites the civilian Chinese philosopher Mencius on the subject of opportunistic warfare:

Those who enriched lands that did not exercise humane government were repudiated by Confucius; how much the more those who aggressively warred for them—fighting for territory, they killed so many people the dead filled the fields; contending for cities, they killed so many people the dead filled the cities. This is what is called leading the land to eat human flesh. Death is not enough for the crime. Therefore those who make war out to be good deserve the supreme penalty.[†]

Naganuma Muneyoshi (1635–1690), a younger contemporary of Yamaga, outlined seven grounds of just warfare: overthrowing brutal tyrants, quelling rebellions against just rule, executing usurpers, stopping factional contests

---

[*] *Ways of Warriors, Codes of Kings,* p. 86.

[†] Cf. *Samurai Wisdom* p. 216.

for power, stopping territorial contention and reuniting a divided nation, avenging national disgrace, and eliminating banditry. In Europe, meanwhile, the work of the Dutch scholar and jurist Hugo Grotius (1583–1645), a forerunner of modern international law, derives the right and duty of self-defense from nature, but conceives of self-defense in an expansive manner that includes acquisition:

> So far from any thing in the principles of nature being repugnant to war, every part of them indeed rather favors it. For the preservation of our lives and persons, which is the end of war, and the possession or acquirement of things necessary and useful to life is most suitable to those principles of nature, and to use force, if necessary, for those occasions, is no way dissonant to the principles of nature, since all animals are endowed with natural strength, sufficient to assist and defend themselves.[‡]

While securing the necessities of life may well be defined as an aspect of self-defense, the problem with this formulation is that wars of acquisition might be rationalized by shortages even if economic difficulties were caused by inefficient domestic policies and practices, or by ineptitude in diplomacy and trade. Such a rationalization of wars of acquisition, like the *lebensraum* argument of National Socialists in twentieth century Germany,

---

[‡] Translated by J.C. Campbell, 1814.

is a classic manipulation of momentum, a way of diverting internal unrest and harnessing it to external aggression. A similar result might be drawn by enterprising interpreters from parts of *Manusmṛti*, a classic text of Hindu law, particularly those pertaining specifically to the chiefs of the *kṣatriya* warrior caste, which bore some resemblance to the Japanese samurai:

> *Chariots and horses, elephants, parasols, money, grain, cattle, women—*
> *all goods, including base metals, belong to he who wins them.*

> *Let the best be given to the king—this is Vedic tradition;*
> *and what has not been won individually is to be given to all the soldiers by the king.*

> *This is declared the impeccable eternal law of warfare:*
> *a warrior killing enemies in battle should not deviate from this.*

> *Let him seek to obtain what has not been obtained;*
> *let him protect what is gained, diligently;*
> *let him increase what is preserved,*
> *and let him distribute to the worthy what has increased.*

> *He should know this four-fold means of attaining human ends;*
> *let him always perform it properly, unwearied, alert.*

What has not been obtained, let him seek by violence;
what has been obtained, let him protect by attention;
what is preserved, let him increase by development;
what has increased, let him distribute to worthy recipients.

Let his mace always be raised,
let his prowess always be evident,
let his secret always be concealed,
let him always go after vulnerabilities.

The whole world trembles before one whose mace is
always raised;
so let him subdue all beings by violence. *

This conception of warfare is close to that propounded by the Prussian militarist Carl von Clausewitz (1780–1831) in his *On War,* considered a classic in the West, where he states unequivocally that, "War is only a part of political discourse."† He also wrote that "Self-imposed restrictions, almost imperceptible and hardly worth mentioning, termed usages of International Law, accompany it without essentially impairing its power."‡ This would seem to tally with the underlying attitude of men like Kansuke's employer Takeda Shingen, hereditary warlords who grew up in a milieu consumed by civil warfare. Insofar as the samurai class was originally constituted to attend to the

---

* Author's translation.
† Translated by J.J. Graham. Penguin Classics edition, p. 402.
‡ Ibid., p. 101.

interests of the aristocracy, such an outlook on war might be expected even if it were not articulated.

The Arts of Warfare are to be Concealed

Because the arts of warfare make deliberate use of change and transformation, secrecy is paramount. Revelation is the same as giving enemies the advantage.

Notes

As noted in the classic *Art of War* by Sun-tzu, tactical misdirection and surprise are essential arts of warfare, which naturally could not operate without the appropriate informational deficits and deceptions.

The *Manusmṛti* says, "Another should not know one's vulnerability, while one should know the other's vulnerability; as a turtle hides its limbs, one should protect one's weaknesses." The Sanskrit strategic classic *Arthaśāstra* of Kauthilya says, "To the extent that a ruler divulges dangerous secrets to people, to that extent, by that act, the independent one becomes subject to control. The works of the unguarded, even if exceptionally successful, will undoubtedly come to naught."*

The primary principles of secrecy and misdirection are common in Chinese military classics. *Master Wei Liao* says, "When you master warfare, you are as though hidden in the earth, as if far out in space, emerging from

---

* Cleary, *The Art of Wealth*, pp. 226-227.

nothing."[†] The *Three Strategies* says, "Without strategy there is no way to settle confusion and doubt; if not for subterfuge and surprise there is no way to defeat treachery and stop enemies; without secret planning there is no way to achieve success."[‡]

Secrecy for the sake of security is also an ancient principle in the Western warrior culture of the Celts. It is given as one of normative prescriptions for chieftains noted in the classic *Councels of Cormac,* an old Irish handbook for princes, where it is paired with a complementary political practice: "Let him be accompanied at conventions, let him be alone at secret councils."[§] The same classic says in respect to reserve and civil security, "A fool is dangerous, a boaster is unguarded, one who is violent is oppressive."[¶]

The Art of War by Niccolò Machiavelli presents an example of the strategic significance of secrecy as well as the reverse exploitation of its compromise by misdirection: If you suspect anybody in your army of giving the enemy intelligence of your designs, you cannot do better than to avail yourself of this treachery by seeming to trust him with some secret resolution which you intend to execute, while you carefully conceal your real design; hence, you may perhaps discover the traitor and lead the enemy into an error that may possibly end in its destruction.[**]

[†] Cleary, *Ways of Warriors, Codes of Kings,* p. 13.

[‡] Ibid. p. 54.

[§] Cleary, *The Counsels of Cormac,* p. 14.

[¶] Ibid. p. 26.

[**] Book Six. Translation by Ellis Farneworth. Da Capo Press, 2001, p. 170.

Traditions of Military Scientists Wearing Confucian Apparel or Monastic Robes

In the arts of war, the tradition of wearing the apparel of a Confucian scholar or a Buddhist monastic is not a fixed standard. In olden times, when Confucians transmitted arts of war to the world, they wore the apparel of scholars; and when Buddhists transmitted the arts of war to the world, they wore religious robes. Later on, in contrast, people who were neither Confucians nor Buddhists taught in the garb of Confucian scholars and Buddhist monks; one does not know the reason for this practice.

Notes

It is not fortuitous that the subject of garb should follow directly on the importance of secrecy. The outward appearances of scholarship or religion may be used malevolently to dissimulate and ingratiate, to gain access to people of power to destroy them or to use them. The message is the need for a leader to find out if the "teacher" is really a Confucian or a Buddhist, implying an ethical or religious person, and not an opportunistic poseur, charlatan, or criminal in disguise.

The Establishment of Schools of the Arts of War

In the art of war it seems there was no such thing as so-and-so's school or such-and-such a school, for it is not seen in the original literature. It is in recent books, such as the *Kōyō Gunkan* and *Kenmon Gunsho* that so-and-so's school, or such-and-such a school, is spoken of. Since then, schools have become even more numerous. To be called "a teacher of the arts of war" and gather students to teach when one has only learned sword techniques is due to basic greed for profit.

To begin with, since the arts of war employ change and transformation, there is no advantage that guarantees certain victory—how can it be assured? What is more, to learn only sword technique to become a teacher of the arts of war is a very shallow interest.

Notes

Essentials of Military Matters critiques the proliferating schools of martial arts more than one hundred years later in peacetime Japan: "Although there are many different systems in the world, they lean toward operation of energy and are insufficiently realistic, they are short on strategy on account of planning, or they attend to mental states and don't apply physical forms, or they have the core but stumble at the outgrowths."*

Transmitters, Practitioners, and Dilettantes of the Arts of War

In the arts of war, there are differences among transmitters, practitioners, and dilettantes.

First, transmitters of arts of war only memorize their teachers' instructions and become teachers and transmit them to disciples without personal application or training.

---

* Cleary, *Samurai Wisdom*, p. 206.

Then, the practitioners are the ones who work and train on the basis of their teachers' instructions and acquire the skills to win every battle.

As for dilettantes, this means people who haven't fully received a teacher's instruction, but manage to develop skills and score a number of successes.

Outside these three, there are the derelicts of the arts of war, those commonly called impetuous and aggressive, or savage brutes. The so-called "art of war" of the impetuous and aggressive is just single-mindedness.

It is precisely those who say there's no use in learning who remain foolish even if single-minded, surviving even where they ought to die and dying even where they ought to survive, ruining their reputations and destroying their families, as has happened to many since olden times.

Note
Surviving where one ought to die implies cowardice, or moral failure; dying where one should survive implies incompetence, or technical failure.

Practice after Learning
Once you have received transmission of arts of war, if you don't recall anything afterward and forget about them, that's equivalent to never having learned. And even if you don't forget anything, if you don't practice them, when the time comes to use them you'll be defenseless. Therefore it is fundamental to practice diligently and train deliberately. Although I practiced this science from the age of

sixteen to thirty, it is because of not yet having mastered military science that I use every event and every thing for assistance.

Notes

This last point, the practice of learning from everything, particularly learning to turn every situation to one's advantage, is one of the key concepts of this school of martial arts, pursued extensively in the works of later practitioners such as the duelist Miyamoto Musashi and the military scientist Yamaga Sokō. *Essentials of Military Matters* explains,

> This system teaches us not to be one-sided, so it takes in what the other is doing, and is also produced from oneself. Even if it is in the action of the other, something that is suitable is adopted and put to use. Whatever is suitable for adoption, be it from events of long ago, or events of the present, and of course the methods of distinguished generals and brave knights, that is taken and put to use, even things from elsewhere or other schools. So anything useful in one's own school, as well as whatever comes from one's own effort and understanding, is all put to use if it should be used.[*]

Something of this strictly strategic approach to military operations is explained in a model dialogue in Yamaga

---

[*] Cleary, *Warrior Wisdom,* p. 202.

Takatsune's *Essentials of Military Matters:* "Question: In this tradition, is the teaching based on ethics and morals, or is it a teaching employing artifice and deception? Answer: In this system both are used, and also not used. Ultimately what must be used is used, what should be left out is left out."* This too is an expression of the art of the advantage, which may require an ethical or moral image with no substance outside of its tactical advantage.

Familiar to modern readers under various names, such as propaganda, perception management, psychological operations, or culture clash, this aspect of warfare was a keen interest of classical writers, and became a specialty of the Takeda establishment, as seen in the extensive *Kōyō Gunkan* dedicated to lionizing the warlord Takeda Shingen. The roles of Buddhism and Christianity in the campaigns of rival warlords Takeda Shingen and Oda Nobunaga afford a prime example of religious affiliations and loyalties being used for purposes of political organization and cultural warfare in pre-modern Japanese history.

The Conduct of the Martial Artist

The conduct of the martial artist is such that whatever is discourteous he does not do, whatever is improper he does not say. He never shows any signs of weakness, but never argues with other people.

These principles are to be kept in mind at all times, in all places, whatever you are doing.

---

* *Samurai Wisdom,* pp. 201-2.

Notes

Because reciprocity is a natural phenomenon as well as a social principle, to be careful of one's face is part of watching one's back, in both civil and military contexts. The seventeenth century Zen master Bankei said, "Samurai always put duty first, and rebuke each other for even a single word out of line, as constant vigilance is the path of the samurai. Once they start rebuking each other they cannot relent, so the sensible thing for people to do all the time is to be careful beforehand to wrap their hard hearts in a soft cover so they don't bump into people in a sharp, edgy manner."[†]

A study of martial arts training for juvenile delinquents in the 1980's compared the results of three approaches. One group was taught an Asian martial art in a traditional manner, including character training; a second group was taught a modern version of the art without the psychological and philosophical element; a third group was used as a control for exercise and contact with the teacher. After six months, the youths in the first group showed lowered levels of aggression and anxiety, and enhanced self-esteem and social skills. The second group showed increased aggressiveness and delinquent tendencies. The third group registered no significant personality effects.[‡]

[†] *Bankei Zenji Hōgo.* Author's translation.
[‡] Michael E. Trulson, "Martial Arts Training: A Novel 'Cure' for Juvenile Delinquency." Human Relations, Vol. 39, No. 12, 1131–1140 (1986)

Soldier as a General Name for Warriors

Military men bear arms, and because they bear arms they are called soldiers. So while *soldier* is a general term for warriors, a general is called an archer, while foot soldiers and those of lesser rank are called troops.

The reasoning for this is that someone qualified to be a general, be it a commander of a hundred men or the commander of a thousand men, is among the troops directing maneuvers. Therefore a commander of a hundred is a hundred men apart, and a commander of a thousand is a thousand men apart, so they cannot direct by manipulations of spear or halberd, sword or dagger; thus they do it with bow and arrow. Because they use bow and arrow, they are called archers.

Even so, winning and losing are the ways of warfare, so it is not only the bow—sometimes wielding a sword, sometimes settling contests with spear or halberd, in any case this can be soldiery. Foot soldiers and below, the horses of war, consider advance to be strength and think falling back is weakness; so they employ weapons all along the continuum of long distance to short range, and thus are called troops.

Notes

The description of infantry as "horses of war" is somewhat more than a metaphor. Advancing without retreating as a fixed aim is in itself neither a sound nor standard principle of strategy, and it is also unnatural. It is, rather, an attitude instilled in order to form a body of men into a weapon, which may itself be destroyed or expended in the process of deployment. Men who thought only of moving forward in battle were people who were trained in this way, like animals trained to obey their masters even in performing actions unnatural to them. This is why these men were drawn from the lower ranks. Here this is depicted in terms neither tragic nor heroic, but professional. This ethos of the professional warrior, uncomplaining dedication and sacrifice, is reflected in the traditional portrait of Yamamoto Kansuke as already maimed by the time he became an infantry commander, eventually to die in combat as an old man.

Martial Arts and Military Science

The reason for distinguishing martial arts and military science is that military science includes skillfully taking castles; securing battle formations in face of enemies; sending signals with pennants, gongs, and drums; mass maneuvers; strategies, tactics and schemes for dealing with strong opponents, weak opponents, big opponents, and small opponents. Martial arts means shooting down those far away, cutting down those nearby, and wrestling to win at close quarters.

These two paths emerge and diverge from one mind. Here I say that the consummation of military science is in martial arts, and the use of martial arts is in military science.

Notes

In his *Book of Five Rings,* Miyamoto Musashi repeatedly refers to mass combat as analogous to individual combat.

Although he was undefeated in individual duels and an heir of the Kansuke school, Musashi did not have the combat experience of Kansuke, who had lived a century earlier during an era of endemic civil war. Even an individual contest is energetically and experientially different when it is happening within a war, so maneuvers that might be executed effectively in a duel in peacetime may not be as practical or efficient in the context of mass combat. This is one reason for the studied simplicity of Kansuke's pragmatic orientation, as compared to the artful elaboration of the schools of swordsmanship that were developed in the era of the urban samurai under the general political stability and peaceful isolation of the Tokugawa regime.

Martial Arts and Medicine

Martial arts and medical arts differ in terms of killing and giving life, but their principle is ultimately one.

Speaking in terms of their difference, martial arts deal with killing, while medical arts deal with fostering life. To be specific, in martial arts, as the enemy is substantial, strategy is used to render him insubstantial to strike him; in medical science, because the patients are depleted, medicine is given to make them substantial to save their lives.

I say that martial arts also deal with life-giving, and medical arts deal with life-giving too, but when misused martial arts also kill, and medical arts kill too.

The fact is that if everyone in society were principled, what would they fight over? If there's no fight, there are no enemies, and if there are no enemies, who would be killed?

In civil society, the people who get killed are the criminals. Because crime is against natural order, thus they become enemies of nature and so destroy themselves.

In the context of medical arts too, if everyone took care of their health, what ailments would they suffer? If they don't get sick, what is there to cure? What is cured is sickness that comes from neglect of health. So does one not perish from sickening one's own body?

When you consider these in terms of their logic, the principles of both paths of giving life and killing are the same.

Notes

The premise that abnormality is a precondition for employment of the arts of warfare as well as the arts of medicine forms the practical basis of professional ethics. The samurai military scientist Muro Naokiyo wrote, "Warfare is not the normal course for sages. It might be called an expedient means. Unless you have expedient means to establish justice, warfare is a difficult path to pursue. In any case, it must be understood that warfare is something distinct, not the normal course of action."*

Arts of War used by Shinto, Confucianism, and Buddhism

The arts of war are used in Shinto, Confucianism, and Buddhism.

Speaking in terms of Shinto, Susano-o no Mikoto drew a sword ten fists long and slew an eight-headed serpent.

---

* Cleary, *Training the Samurai Mind,* p. 105.

Speaking in terms of Confucianism, Confucius wielded an eighteen-inch sword and the crooked retreated.

Speaking in terms of Buddhism, the Imperturbable One conquers evil devils with a keen sword. Also, the eulogies of the great sage Kinnara king says, "I've heard bodhisattvas stay in the world to show compassion—how can they project ferocity to govern by awe? Only if the compassionate are brave are they the support of humanity and nature with a staff and a shout when devil banditti act at will in the world, causing alienation."

Notes

Even military scientists living in times of war and personally immersed in the arts of war typically sought some sort of moral justification for the use of arms, even if only that the ancestors, ancients, deities, or heroes of old used arms. The argument from traditional precedent is a normative proxy for the argument of preservation of a civilization, and military scientists in feudal Japan set forth a variety of justifications for military action. While these are generally framed in terms of protecting society from internal and external threats and disturbances, there have also been some writers on the subject who celebrate militancy and martial prowess per se, as the quintessence of a warrior. Diametrically opposed opinions of the military adventures of the hegemon Toyotomi Hideyoshi are useful illustrations of the immense difference among moral and political viewpoints within the spectrum of the Japanese warrior culture of Bushidō. According to Satō Nobuhiro

(1773–1850), a specialist in agricultural administration writing in a time of growing apprehension about the intentions of European powers in Asia,

> Until two hundred years ago, myriad nations trembled in fear of Japan's military threat. Basically, the men of those times were all trained in military affairs and were extremely bold and fierce in bloody combat, so even the foreigners in Western countries had heard of our reputation, and to this day they still cannot try anything because of that residual threat. Considered from this point of view, I realize that Hideyoshi's attack on Korea was in infinitely great achievement for the whole country of Japan. Magnificent![*]

In contrast, the earlier military scientist Muro Naokiyo (1658–1734), an attendant lecturer and consultant to the Shogun when the national isolation policy seemed secure and Japan was unusually peaceful and prosperous, took a dim moral view of Hideyoshi's undoubted martial prowess:

> Although Toyotomi Hideyoshi was inhumane and didn't make war to punish the violent and stop disorder, because he understood the major calculations of victory and defeat he would launch military expeditions without effort, deploying his troops

---

[*] *Training the Samurai Mind,* p. 221.

without any clever planning. When it came to combat, he would always succeed in a single onslaught. I've never heard of him taking time off from warfare. He was close to those who though unskilled are quick. His tactics as a commander may have been beyond Uesugi Kenshin and Takeda Shingen, but as a hasty, crafty, and cruel man, he couldn't even dream of manners, music, kindness, and love. So in his later years he raised an army without honor to invade Korea; as he kept the troops in the field for a long time and massacred the populace, the hearts of everyone in the world turned against him.[*]

Five Curricula of the Arts of War

In the arts of war there are what are called five curricula. First is the advantageous uses of weaponry. Second is the advantageous uses of personnel. Third is the advantageous uses of terrain. Fourth is the advantageous uses of the weather. Fifth is the advantageous uses of assistance.

These five curricula are outlined in this book, called *The Book of Secrets of the Arts of War*.

Note

The advantageous uses of assistance refers back to the conclusion of section 11, "I use every event and every thing for assistance."

---

[*] *Training the Samurai Mind*, p. 104.

PART II

Wrestling

Wrestling and Boxing

To begin with, the two arts of wrestling and boxing are not arts for major war, but even so, when you learn these methods, they have great advantages for limbering the body, so you can advance when you should and retreat when you should, and settle contests grappling. So as a primer of martial arts for beginners, in my leisure I've had an artist draw pictures of forms of those two arts. There are so many that I've shown the general outlines, dividing yang and yin forms. The principles of these forms, furthermore, can be adapted to all sorts of changes.

Notes

"Wrestling" is used as a term of convenience, although it is too crude for the term *keisei* used here, which is more descriptive of the essence of the art and literally means *giving form to momentum.* While the sense and general principles of giving form to momentum are fairly obvious in the physical realm, in a broader context giving form to momentum may be considered a quintessential mechanism of the art of the advantage, a master key to leadership and power as well as to exploitation, manipulation, and underhanded proceedings of all kinds.

Yang Forms

Figure B   Figure A

When A tries to hit B with his right hand, B makes as if to hit A with his left, but instead of striking, he puts his left hand on A's chest, puts his left foot behind A, and with his right hand grabs A's calf to throw him.

Also, when A tries to hit B with his right hand, B makes as if to hit A with his left, but instead of striking, B places his left foot behind A, then reaches around A's shins and lifts both of A's feet to throw him.

If A is coming on too strong to lift his feet, then B can throw him by dropping down onto his back in front of A.

Yin Forms

Figure B   Figure A

When A tries to hit B with his right hand, B makes as if to block it with his left, then immediately grabs A by the chest with his left hand, turns his body into him, and lifts A's leg with his right hand to throw him forward.

When A tries to hit B with his right hand, B makes as if to block it with his left, then ducks down in front of A, puts his hands around A's calves, then pulls forward and up to throw him.

Encounter

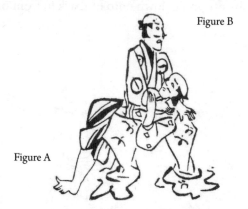

Figure B

Figure A

As A is coming along unwary, B acts as if he is passing by, then grabs A by the throat with his right hand and puts his left hand to the small of A's back to lay him down as in the illustration.

Variation:
If B is about to be lain down, B can grab and hang onto A's left arm with both hands to get up.

Grappling

Figure B   Figure A

When B grabs A's chest with his left hand and tries to stab him with a dagger in his right, A grabs B's left arm as in the illustration, shifts behind B, and arrests his incipient stab with his right hand.

Variation:
If B breaks the hand held by A free with his leg and tries to stab, A regains the advantage by pressing him down to stop him.

Grappling When on Your Back

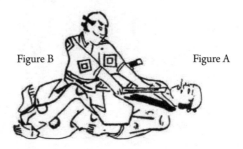

Figure B   Figure A

A is on his back, as in the illustration; B seizes him by the chest with his left hand and holds a dagger to his chest with his right. A gets the advantage by sweeping B's dagger away with his hand and pushing B off with his foot to get up.

Drawing Swords

In the matter of drawing swords, you have to be careful about how you wear your sash. When your sash is tight, it's comfortable to wear swords in it, but the blades are close to your body. But then if you loosen it, the blades are away from your body but wearing the swords in your sash is uncomfortable. Therefore it's best for the sash not to be too tight or too loose. The sash should be lowered with the left hand, not hiked up. Swords should be drawn to the right with the right hand, not drawn forward. The scabbard should be held down with the left hand, not raised. The lower leg should be drawn out of the way on the left, not extended. The left leg should be pulled back, not extended.

Frontal Check

Figure B   Figure A

When A is about to draw his sword, B arrests A's drawing hand. A may break B's grip with the sword handle and try to draw, or may pivot to the left, standing up his shin to knock B's hand off with that shin and draw.

Variation:
If B's hand is knocked away and the hand is tied up, then B can put his left hand on A's shoulder and stick his left foot in A's back left side to push him down.

Sword Check

Figure B   Figure A

As A is about to draw his sword, B seizes the hilt of A's sword with his right hand and takes the tip of the scabbard in his left hand; with his left foot, B steps behind A's right side to throw him backward, as in the illustration.

Variation:
When A has been thrown backward, it is advantageous for him to throw his weight forward. Then B can take advantage of that by dropping down in front of A to throw him over.

Check from Behind

Whenever someone comes from behind and grabs the sword and dagger of someone in front of him, as in the illustration, the one in front can grab the hands of the one behind him, pull them up, then duck down to throw him over his shoulders.

Variation:
When the one behind is being thrown by the one in front, he can grab the one in front by the chest and throw the one who threw him, over his shoulders.

PART III

Swordsmanship

On Swords and Swordsmanship

Now then, the swords used by warriors are like the fangs of ferocious beasts. If tigers and wolves had no fangs, how would they differ from horses and oxen? Samurai too, because they wear swords, differ from farmers, artisans, merchants, and entertainers, constituting a power able to maintain arms.

Among the capable commanders of Japan and China on whom we have information, some knew swordsmanship by nature, some learned it by study, and some learned it through struggle. In order to illustrate the main principles, I have engaged an artist; but since the myriad changes and alternatives cannot be drawn, I've had him depict the stance as the beginning, then striking, parrying, and cutting. For those who master the principles, what variations will be beyond their function?

Even Overhead Sword-Backward Posture

When taking this posture, you should strike straight, moving in when the opponent, sword raised, is not yet expecting it.

If the adversary steps in first trying to hit you, watch his sword come out; withdraw your left torso and leg, and strike his hand as he lashes out.

If the adversary tries to sweep-slash you horizontally below, strike him in the same way as the foregoing scenario.

If the opponent comes moving in with his sword pointing forward at midlevel, switch to a stance with your sword cocked to the lower right pointing forward.

In a contest where you and an adversary both have your swords in upper positions, you can get the advantage by leaping to your adversary's right in order to strike.

When the adversary holds his sword to the lower right pointing forward or to the lower left pointing forward, judgment of space is of paramount importance. You must discern the advantages of each party; don't take the view that when the adversary is in a yin position and you are in a yang position then yin turns out yang and yang turns out yin.

Notes

This last admonition means that the principle of yin and yang interchanging cannot be transferred from abstraction into practice in an automatic way, as the advantages of each party in every particular situation have to be calculated concretely. The yin and yang factors of a situation in its totality are not necessarily aligned or apportioned evenly, either by the positions or the maneuvers of participating parties, so an oversimplified formula applied to a partial assessment can easily have unforeseen consequences.

The term for sweep-slash, *nagu,* when not written in *kana* in this text, is written with an *ateji* or ad-hoc homonym, in this case one that means *throw.* The Japanese word *nagu* here is the same as in *nagi-nata,* the halberd, though the Chinese characters used are different. The use of simpler *ateji* for more complicated originals is characteristic of this genre of Japanese for a number of historical reasons, but in this case the physical possibility of throwing a sword could lead to confusion about the meaning of the text if taken literally. Throwing a sword is expressed by a distinct technical term, and is in any case not indicated in these particular maneuvers. The word used for the low horizontal sweep-slash, readily associated with a halberd, comes by analogy from a character used for the action of the scythe.

Right Upper Sword-Backward Posture

This stance is advantageous to strike unexpectedly when an adversary is poised with his sword raised.

There's an advantage when an adversary steps in first to try to hit you.

There's an advantage when an adversary tries to sweep-slash you sideways low.

There's an advantage when an adversary moves in with his sword straight out in the center.

The advantages in these four cases are the same as the advantages of the even overhead back-pointing sword posture.

When an adversary is calculating advantage, not moving, you change your sword position to make the opponent's eyes and mind move; then, calculating advantage, strike. This technique can be used with any stance.

When an adversary comes with his sword to his lower left pointing forward, by holding your sword tip downward you can get the advantage by striking upwards with both hands.

Sword Held Cross-Hand Even Overhead Pointing Forward

This stance is advantageous against an opponent wielding his sword in an upper position in a moment of inattention.

There's an advantage when the adversary steps in first to try to strike you.

There's an advantage when the adversary tries to sweep-slash you horizontally low.

There's an advantage when the adversary comes moving in with his sword level in the middle pointing forwards.

The advantages in these four cases are the same as the advantages of the even overhead sword-backward posture.

There's an advantage when an adversary is motionless calculating advantage. There's an advantage when an opponent comes with his sword cocked to the lower left pointing forward.

These two cases are the same as the advantages of the left upper back-pointing sword.

When an adversary comes moving in with his sword pointing forward level in the middle, the rule is to switch your own stance so your sword is cocked to the lower right pointing forward. It's also advantageous to sweep aside the opponent's sword and move right in.

Stance with Sword Held Cross-Hand Forward to the Upper Left

This stance is advantageous against an adversary with his sword in an upper position in a moment of inattention.

There's an advantage when an adversary steps in first to hit you.

There's an advantage when an adversary tries to sweep-slash you low.

There's an advantage when an opponent comes moving in with his sword even pointing forward in the middle.

In these four cases, the advantages are the same as the aforementioned advantages of the sword held to the right upper rear.

There's an advantage when an adversary is calculating advantage and not moving.

There's an advantage when an adversary comes on with his sword forward to the lower right.

In these two cases, the advantages are the same as the advantages of the sword to the right upper rear.

When an adversary does not calculate advantage, but just rushes right in to strike with the intention to settle the contest with one stroke, there is advantage in moving in to stop him. There is also advantage in jumping over behind the adversary to his left to strike him.

Left Upper Sword-Forward Position

When you're poised in this posture and an adversary with his sword in an upper position tries to strike your right shoulder, you watch the line of his sword, sidestep to the adversary's right, and strike the adversary's hand as he lashes out.

When an adversary with his sword in an upper position tries to hit your poised hands, the adversary's sword can miss its aim; carefully watching the adversary's sword coming out, move in to strike.

When an adversary tries to sweep-slash you low, carefully watch his sword come out, draw back your right foot, and hit his hand lashing out.

When an adversary holds his sword in a lower position and tries to sweep your hands, carefully watch his sword coming out and move in to stab him.

Even Upper Sword-Forward Posture

When poised this way, there is an advantage against an adversary poised in an upper position, in a moment of inattention.

There is an advantage when an adversary tries to strike you first.

There is an advantage when an opponent tries to sweep low first.

In these three cases, the advantages are the same as those with the sword held cross-hand forward to the right at midlevel.

When an adversary comes with his sword forward even at midlevel, there is advantage in moving right in defensively. It's also good to shift your sword to lower right cross-hand forward-pointing position.

Sword Forward Middle Right Cross-Hand Posture

When poised in this way, there is advantage in moving directly in when the adversary is in an upper position, in a moment of inattention.

If the adversary tries to strike your face or shoulder first, draw back your left torso and leg and hit the adversary's hands as he lashes out.

If the adversary tries to sweep low first, strike with the same technique as the foregoing.

When you and an adversary make to move in on each other with the same sword position, the advantage is the same, while disparity in the advantage of above and below of the points is inauspicious.

The adversary tries to strike your face or your shoulder: while ready to parry with your sword, it is advantageous to jump to the adversary's back left side and strike.

Left Middle Sword-Forward Posture

When poised like this, when the adversary is in an upper position, in a moment of inattention you should strike moving straight in.

When the adversary tries to hit you first, there is advantage in sidestepping to the adversary's right and striking.

If the adversary tries to sweep you low first, you can get the advantage by drawing back your right foot and hitting the adversary's hands as he lashes out.

If the adversary comes on with his sword in a middle position, there is advantage in tying him up and crowding in.

Even Middle Upraised Sword Posture

There is advantage in this position when an adversary is momentarily inattentive in an upper position.

There is advantage when the adversary tries to hit you first.

There is advantage when the adversary tries to sweep you low first.

The foregoing three cases are the same as with the sword cocked cross-hand to the right in a middle position pointing forward.

When an adversary comes on with this sword in a middle position, there is advantage in switching yours to a lower position.

When an adversary comes on with his sword in a lower position, there is advantage in moving in blocking with your point downward.

Even Middle Level Sword-Forward Posture

There is advantage in this position when an adversary in an upper position is momentarily inattentive.

There is advantage when the adversary tries to hit you first.

There is advantage when the adversary tries to sweep you low.

In these three cases the advantages are the same as the even middle level upraised sword position.

When the adversary tries to hit you first, there is advantage in moving straight in.

If the adversary comes on with his sword in a lower position, there is advantage in moving in blocking with your sword tip down.

When an adversary tries to hit you first, there is advantage in sidestepping to the adversary's right to move in.

Right Lower Sword-Backward Posture

In this posture, there is advantage in moving straight in when the adversary is not expecting it.

If the adversary tries to strike first, there is advantage in drawing back your left foot and hitting the opponent's hands as he lashes out.

When an adversary comes on with his sword in a middle position, you can get the advantage by switching your sword to left lower back position.

Sword-Forward Lower Left Cross-Hand Posture

In this posture, if an adversary tries to hit you first, there is advantage in parrying moving in. There is also advantage in blocking. There is also advantage in sidestepping to the right and striking.

If the adversary tries to sweep-slash low, there is advantage in drawing back your left foot and cutting the opponent's hands as he sweeps.

If the adversary comes on with his sword in a middle position, there is advantage in parrying and moving in.

Sword-Forward Lower Right Cross-Hand Posture

In this posture, there is advantage in moving directly in as an adversary is raising his sword to an upper position and is unready.

If the opponent tries to sweep-slash first, there is advantage in drawing back to strike. There is also advantage in immediately moving in. There is also advantage in drawing back then moving in.

If the adversary tries to hit you first, there is advantage in diverting the force to the adversary's left.

If the adversary comes on with his sword in a middle position, there is advantage in moving in blocking, and there is also advantage in moving in parrying.

Lower Right Sword-Forward Posture

In this posture, there is advantage in moving directly in when the adversary is not expecting it.

If the adversary tries to strike first, there is advantage in moving in blocking, and also advantage in moving in tying him up.

If the adversary tries to sweep-slash first from the left, there is advantage in drawing your leg back to strike.

Sword Backward to the Lower Left, Cross-Hand

When in this posture, if an adversary tries to hit you from an upper level position, you draw back your right foot and hit the opponent's hand as he lashes out.

If the opponent comes on with his sword in a middle position, there is advantage in moving in blocking.

If the opponent tries to sweep–slash low first, your advantage is the same as in the corresponding position to the right side.

Separated Sword Position—Short Above, Long Below

When you're in this posture and an adversary tries to strike you first, there is advantage in drawing back your left and striking with your right. Also, the same advantage is there when the adversary tries to sweep-slash low.

When an adversary just postures and does not lash out, you can get the advantage by using your short sword to move the opponent's eyes and get him to lash out with his sword.

Swords Forward: Short Above, Long Below

There is advantage in this position when an adversary tries to strike first.

There is advantage when an opponent tries to sweep-slash low first.

These two cases are the same as the separated sword position with the short sword above and the long sword below.

When the adversary tries to sweep-slash below first, it is advantageous to stop the adversary's sword with your long sword and strike with your short sword.

Long and Short Swords Crossed Forward Position

When in this position, when an adversary tries to strike, it is advantageous to block with your short sword and strike with your long sword.

If the adversary tries to sweep-slash low first, stopping the adversary's long sword with your long sword, you can get the advantage with your short sword.

If the adversary shifts from upper to middle to lower position to make your eyes move, you should go in directly when you see an opening. Also, when the adversary is not moving but calculating advantage, you get the advantage using your short sword as a projectile.

Same Positions

In this case, when an adversary tries to sweep-slash below, there is advantage in immediately cutting the adversary's hands.

Also, there is advantage in moving directly in when the adversary draws back his sword.

There is also advantage in moving directly in when the adversary tries to strike your right side.

Slipping and Blocking with the Sword

In this position, you should stab moving straight in.

If the adversary tries to sweep-slash low, you should draw back your left foot and immediately cut the adversary's hands.

When the adversary is about to draw back his sword, you should slash moving right in.

Moving in Blocking with the Sword

In this situation, pressing up close and grabbing the adversary's hand with your left hand, you can get the advantage with your right.

If the adversary tries to sweep low, you draw back your left and cut the opponent's sweeping hands.

When the adversary is drawing back his sword, you should move right in and strike.

Strike Moving In

Strike Pulling Back

Slipping Strike

Blocking Strike

PART IV

The Pole

The Chief of the Arts

The pole is the chief of the arts. The explanation for this is that, for the spear and the halberd techniques, you cannot do without the pole too. So those who would acquire the techniques of long weapons first make this art the basis, learning the ways of using the body, hands, and feet, so they might attain the expert use of all the weapons in a warrior's arsenal. Based on these principles, I've had illustrations made to show beginners, none but those for which one pattern applies to myriad patterns.

The pole is approximately eight to eight and a half feet long.

High Even All Around Pole Position

When in this position (there are three levels—high, middle, and lower), there is advantage in jabbing and there is advantage in hitting when the adversary is not expecting it.

If the adversary tries to hit you first, there is advantage in drawing back your left and striking with the right.

If the adversary tries to sweep you low first, there is advantage in pulling back the left and putting forth the right, to stop the opponent's pole and jab or strike.

If the adversary tries to jab from an upper or middle position, there is advantage in ducking rearward to jab underneath.

The foregoing techniques are not limited to the pole, but are the same with any weapon.

Sword-Drawing Pole Position

When in this position, there is advantage in sweeping when the opponent isn't expecting it, and there is advantage in hitting.

When the adversary tries to strike first, there is advantage in deflecting the adversary's pole upward, and then jabbing straight.

When an adversary tries to sweep low first, there is advantage in leaping away and striking the adversary's sweeping hands, and there is also advantage in ducking out of the way and jabbing.

When an adversary tries to jab you first, there is advantage in shifting your body to make the adversary's pole go over your shoulder and then jabbing straight.

Wielding the Pole in One Hand

In this position, there is advantage in jabbing and striking when the adversary isn't expecting it.

If an adversary tries to sweep low first, there is advantage in knocking away the adversary's pole and jabbing.

If the adversary strikes first, there is advantage in withdrawing your left and putting forth your right to strike.

If the adversary tries to strike first, there is advantage in slipping his pole to the left and jabbing.

"Thorn Used Backwards" Pole Position

In this position there is advantage in sweeping and there is advantage in striking—when the adversary is not expecting it.

If the adversary tries to sweep low first, there is advantage in drawing back your left to sweep.

"Carrying a Mountain on Your Back" Pole Position

In this posture, there is advantage in striking and there is advantage in sweeping—when the adversary is not expecting it.

If the adversary tries to strike first, there is advantage in pulling back your left and striking, bringing the pole down from your shoulder with your right hand.

If the adversary tries to sweep first, the advantage is the same idea as the foregoing.

If he comes on in a middle position, there is advantage in sweeping the opponent low.

"Handful of Gold" Pole Position

In this posture, there is advantage in striking and there is advantage in sweeping—when the adversary is not expecting it.

If the adversary tries to sweep low first, there is advantage in pulling back your right and hitting the adversary's hand.

Variation

If the adversary pulls back as you hit, you don't land; then there is advantage in moving directly in, jabbing.

If the adversary tries to sweep your pole aside, there is advantage in pulling your pole back so that the adversary's pole misses, then moving in.

PART V

The Spear

The King of Weapons

Overall, the spear is technically the king of weapons, hard to oppose by other weapons. When applying the arts of warfare, whether establishing understanding of all the weapons, or evaluating the relative strength and gravity of captains by your own power, you should practice arresting, blocking, lifting, grabbing, and dodging, and grasp the essential advantages inside, outside, above, in the middle, and below.

Now then, when it comes time to stab, if your aim is off you won't get to the adversary, and if you miscalculate the distance you'll lose. So unless you understand emptiness and fullness in straightforward and surprise tactics, know the limits before and behind, left and right, understand the strengths and weaknesses of others and self, host and guest, and can think clearly and effectively in an instant, how could anyone comprehend this path?

Left Middle Spear Position

This position is advantageous for stabbing directly when the adversary is off guard.

When an adversary tries to stab first in an upper position, it is advantageous to duck under the adversary's spear to stab him.

The foregoing advantages are the same with either a sword or a halberd.

If the adversary tries to sweep with a halberd first, it is advantageous to lower your spear tip to stop the adversary's halberd, and when the adversary draws back his halberd it is advantageous to move directly in.

If an adversary tries to brush away the spear you're wielding, there is advantage in neutralizing the adversary's weapon to move in, and there is also advantage in moving directly in.

Notes

The word for neutralizing, *nuku,* can mean to pull, and also to slip (past). This can refer to seizing and pulling the opponent's spear to neutralize the weapon, throw the adversary off balance, and move in; or it can refer to slipping the adversary's spear, which is thus internally deflected by the momentum of his attempt to brush aside the opposing spear, and thus moving in through this opening.

The word for off guard, *fui,* means mentally off guard, whether or not physically poised. To make a move when the adversary is off guard means to act when the adversary isn't anticipating or expecting it, or isn't perceptually prepared or fully mentally present even if he is physically on guard at a given moment as a matter of course in a fight. One of the specific uses of the general tactic of waiting calmly for an adversary to act is to fatigue the opposition in the brain as well as the body, causing neurological tension to mount beyond a certain threshold so as to induce a break in sustained attention or an eruption into uncontrolled action, thus exposing the adversary to preemption or counterattack.

Spears in the Same Position

In this position, there is advantage in spearing directly when the adversary is not expecting it.

When the adversary tries to spear you first, there is advantage in dodging and spearing.

When you and an adversary are both weakening, there is advantage in making a show of lowering your spear tip and then, when the enemy tries to move in, you spear him.

Middle to Lower Spear Position

Figure B   Figure A

If A tries to spear first, B's advantage is in deflecting it upward with his own spear, and then stabbing.

If B tries to spear first, A's advantage is in stabbing with his spear slightly lowered.

If either A or B tries to maneuver with deep thrusts of the spear, for the one who is being maneuvered, the advantage is in spearing directly.

Upper and Middle Spear Position

Figure B   Figure A

In these positions there is advantage for either in spearing the other when he is off guard.

If A tries to spear B in the right side first, B's advantage is in spearing directly, and there is also advantage in dodging to the right and spearing.

If B tries to spear A's right side first, A's advantage is in dodging to the right and spearing.

If B tries to spear A low first, A's advantage is in spearing B in the abdomen through the positions of his hands.

Note

In the last move noted here, when B tries to spear A low, B's arms are extended with hands below shoulder level, exposing B's abdomen to a spear thrust through the gap between B's arms.

Mutual Spearing Position

When your spears are crossed like this, when the adversary pulls back your advantage is in spearing directly.

If the adversary tries to spear low, your advantage is in spearing straight on.

If the adversary tries to stick you, your advantage is in dodging and striking.

If the adversary rushes at you to spear you, your advantage is in leaning in and sinking down to spear him.

Raised and Lowered Spear Positions

Figure B   Figure A

A is in yin position, B is in yang position. For yang, there is advantage in jabbing first. For yin there is advantage in counter-jabbing.

For the sake of learners I don't indicate the principles inflexibly; strategic adaptation is necessary.

Upraised Crossed Spear Position

With spears crossed like this, if the adversary pulls back, your advantage is in stabbing directly.

If the adversary tries to stab you, your advantage is in dodging and stabbing. There is also advantage in stabbing directly.

If the adversary tries to stab you low, your advantage is in stabbing straight.

Outside-Inside Spear Positions

Figure B   Figure A

If B tries to stab first this way, A's advantage is in deflecting it upward over his shoulder and then stabbing straight.

When B goes to draw back his spear, A's advantage is in stabbing in concert with his spear.

Lower Crossed Spear Position

When spears are crossed like this, if the adversary pulls back, your advantage is in stabbing straight on.

If the adversary tries to stab you, your advantage is in slipping his spear and thrusting.

If the adversary tries to stab you from above, your advantage is to duck, block, and thrust defensively.

When the adversary tries to stab you, it is to your advantage to hit the adversary's hands with the butt end of your spear.

Spear vs. Hooked Spear

Figure B   Figure A

When spears are crossed like this, A has the advantage. That advantage is in the way that B cannot advance without withdrawing, and cannot stab without disengaging. Therefore, if B tries to pull back, A has the advantage in thrusting directly. If B tries to disengage, A has the advantage in stabbing him immediately in the body. The rest is transmitted in person.

Spear vs. Trident

Figure B   Figure A

If A tries to arrest B's spear, B's advantage is in stabbing directly.

If B tries to break loose, A's advantage is in stabbing directly moving in.

Standing Rock Posture

In this position, there is advantage in stabbing directly when the adversary is off guard.

If an adversary draws his weapon first, it is to your advantage to stab directly defensively.

If the adversary tries to sweep low first, your advantage is in dodging to stab him in the gut opposite; and it is also advantageous to cut off his hands.

If an adversary goes for his sword, it is advantageous for you to rush at him; and if the adversary takes advantage of a gap to move in on you, it is advantageous for you to hit the adversary's hands with the butt end of your weapon.

High Mountain Position

In this position it is advantageous to thrust at an adversary directly when he is off guard.

If an adversary tries to close in with a halberd, it is advantageous for you to thrust directly; and it is also advantageous to hit his hands with the butt end of your weapon.

If the adversary tries to sweep low first, it is advantageous to back out of the way and cut his hands.

When the adversary thrusts with a spear, it is advantageous to deflect it upward with the butt end of your weapon and try to stab him; then when the adversary makes to withdraw, it is advantageous to cut him with your blade end.

PART VI

Archery

One of the Six Arts

Archery is one of the six arts. It can destroy enemies at a distance without cutting, without combat; burn down citadels and strongholds all at once—ultimately, since the measure is in the skill of your two hands, who could take this art lightly? It's just a matter of developing skill over time, so that you may gradually master it.

Notes

This segment provides no technique, and is concerned with gauging aim according to distance. The original chart is inconsistent, including lesser elevations for longer distances, and in any case is of no practical use as a general guide as it has no specifications of bow pull or other conditions necessary to gauge trajectory, its sole concern.

Thus the text itself states that there are various verbal instructions.

The text also gives an ordinary formula for black powder for incendiary arrows, forty parts saltpeter to twenty-nine parts sulfur and ten parts carbon black. Yamamoto evinces nothing of the reservations of the Chinese classic *Art of War* by Sun Tzu regarding the use of fire as a weapon. Some two hundred years after this text was composed, the St. Petersburg Declaration of 1868 renounced the use of explosive projectiles under 400 grams in weight in wartime, as causes of excessive and unnecessary suffering. While neither Japan nor the United States were among the nineteen signatories to the St. Petersburg Declaration, it created a precedent for prohibition of particular means of warfare at the Hague Peace Conferences of 1899 and 1907. The charge for an incendiary arrow recommended in Yamamoto's instructions is approximately 11.25 grams.

PART VII

Firearms

Instruments of Killing

Guns came to Japan in 1501, and spread everywhere in the Tenbun era [1532–55]. So there is no rule for them in traditional military science. Nevertheless, in view of their function as instruments of killing and wounding, samurai have no business ignoring them.

Notes

The brief technical part of the text that follows in the original is confined to range-finding for chain volleying, including the appropriate musket charges. It is outdated in respect to most parameters of firepower, but the damage done to human bodies by readily deformed musket balls could actually be greater than that inflicted by jacketed bullets of later times. According to *Tactics,* a German manual of tactics translated for the American military, during the Russo-Japanese war of

1904–5, men with bullet wounds to the chest were walking to aid stations, albeit complaining of breathing difficulties. When obstructions cause jacketed bullets to tumble, or cause the jackets to rupture and expose the lead core, the damage done to a human (and, as the aforementioned manual also notes, to animals) is greater and more grievous. The bullets used by the Russians were larger than the Japanese bullets, and the wounds they caused required longer healing time, but neither had the destructive power of modern weapons. According to *Tactics*, "The ballistic advantage of a small-caliber projectile (undesirable from a military surgeon's point of view) have been obtained by the adoption of a point-nose bullet (called the "S" bullet in Germany and the "D" bullet in France). A further advantage of these bullets is that they produce serious wounds on account of their tendency to tumble. These wounds, while not inhuman, instantly disable the man struck, or, at any rate, postpone his recovery indefinitely."* A decisive factor in Japan's favor in the Russo-Japanese war is said to have been medical rather than martial in nature, but not merely by virtue of treatment of wounds. *Seirogan,* "the pill that beat Russia," is a creosote-based palliative for gastrointestinal disorders of the sort that would commonly put personnel out of commission. By WWII, Japanese medical science was dominated by martial concerns, devoted to the development of biological weaponry and discovery of the limits of human capacity to endure inhuman atrocities.[†]

---

* Balck, *Tactics.* Translated by Walter Krueger, 1915.

† Cf. Gold, H. *Unit 731 Testimony.* Tokyo, Yenbooks, 1996.

PART VIII

Human Advantages

Spirit and Mind

Major military science is all a matter of principles. What knows those principles is mind. What leads mind is spirit.

Spirit may be clear or clouded; mind may be intelligent or foolish. What is clouded and foolish is ignorant of everything.

For this reason, the principles of spirit and mind are noted first in reference to human advantages, to make this clear.

The Undefiled One said,

This round mind-mirror originally has no dust;
Because of dust, it cannot reflect original reality.
When the dust is gone, the mirror's clear, not a single thing
    there;
Naturally it shows the body of the Dharma King.

Notes

The word for spirit used here, *ki*, referring to the psychological state, is variously glossed as spirit, mind, heart, intention, will, and mood. It has the primitive and general meaning of energy of any kind, mental or physical, and is used in many compounds such as *ki-bun*, mood or frame of mind; *ki-gokoro*, disposition or temperament; *ki-ryoku*, energy, vigor, mettle, spirit; *ki-baru*, to exert oneself. The effect of mood on physical performance was well known to traditional military scientists, and mood cultivation was part of samurai training. Yamaga Sokō of the same school writes in his work *The Way of the Knight*, "Because the mind depends on the mood, when your mood is calm your mind is calm. When your mood is agitated, then your mind is agitated. Since the mind and the mood are not in two separate states, there is no disparity between them. As the mood exteriorizes the agitation of the mind within, cultivating your disposition should be considered the basis of personal refinement and soundness of mind."*

Yin and Yang, Strength and Weakness

In assessing adversaries, there are distinctions of yin and yang, strength and weakness.

First, a yin opponent is calm and outwardly appears weak, but in the event has strength.

A yang opponent is agitated and outwardly appears strong, but in the event has weakness.

---

* Cleary, *Samurai Wisdom*, p. 38.

Even so, since changing is a function of military science, you project false impressions of strength and weakness. Therefore they are not used as fixed definitions.

Notes

The Chinese strategic classic *The Master of Demon Valley* uses parallel concepts of yin and yang to apply more generally to analogous tactical adaptation of behavior:

> The course of opening and closing is proven by yin and yang. When speaking with those who are in a yang mode, go by the exalted and the lofty; when speaking with those who are in a yin mode, go by the humble and the small. Seek the small by lowliness, seek the great by loftiness. Follow this procedure, and what you say can be expressed anywhere, will penetrate anywhere, and can suit any situation. It will thereby be possible to persuade individuals, to persuade families, to persuade nations, to persuade the world....
>
> The concrete expressions of increase and reduction, rejection and acceptance, opposition and reversion, are all controlled by yin and yang. Yang is mobile and active; yin is still and unobtrusive. When yang emerges in activity, yin accordingly goes into concealment. When yang comes to an end, it returns to the beginning; and when yin reaches a climax, it reverts to yang.[†]

[†] Cleary, *Thunder in the Sky,* pp. 6–7.

The Chinese military classic *Three Strategies* also illustrates this type of tactical adaptation:

> The soft can overcome the hard, the weak can overcome the strong. Softness is benign, hardness is malignant. The weak are helped by others; the strong are attacked by enemies. There is a place to feign weakness, a place to exercise hardness, a place to employ weakness, and a place to apply strength. Include all four, and use whichever is best according to the circumstances.
>
> If it can be soft and can be hard, that country will increasingly flourish. If it can be weak and can be strong, that country will increasingly thrive. If it is only soft or only weak, that country will deteriorate. If it is only hard or only strong, that country will perish.[*]

One Mind, Two Bodies

The principle of one eye, two minds, and three legs orally transmitted in military science means seeing the adversary's state with your eyes, figuring how to win in your mind, and on that basis jumping in, stepping in, or rushing in to strike the adversary.

When it is told this way, it seems like a three-step process, so I teach it as *one mind, two bodies*. To be specific, the eyes see from the mind, and the feet step from the

---

[*] Cleary, *Ways of Warriors, Codes of Kings*, p. 42.

mind too. For this reason I don't express them separately but refer to them together as *one mind.*

Also, the body is the house of the mind, which has no distinct substance apart from the body. The eyes are also in the body, and the hands and feet are in the body too, so I call it *two bodies.*

Someone argues, "The body only works with mind; so what is the logic of distinguishing them?" I reply that there are two considerations here. One is the matter of substance and function, the other is the sense of knowledge and action. For this reason I teach it as one mind, two bodies.

Notes

Unification of mind and body is an active element of expertise in martial arts, manual labor, craft, mime, theater, dance, athletics, and healing. In Asia, this is one reason for the use of traditional meditation techniques by people of many professions, to enhance their functional capacities by mind-body unification methods.

The concept of mind as a second body introduced here is not commonly expressed in this manner, and therefore is of particular interest. Just as the body has a head, hands, and feet, so the mind has intellect, will, and emotion. Just as the body has form, movement, and location, consciousness has cognitive configurations and boundaries, and attention both travels and tarries.

The phenomenon known in the Japanese language as *kehai,* literally meaning energy distribution, is also suggested by the second mental body to which Kansuke refers.

The manipulation of one's own energy field, and the perception of others' energy fields, is an essential skill in Japanese culture, not only in martial arts, but in the acceptable organization of spatial, sensual, perceptual, and psychological relations within the restrictions of compulsory coexistence.

Many misunderstandings may arise in the course of interaction of energy fields under conditions of comparative chaos such as those occasioned by releases that are interpreted differently by interacting parties according to the way the mind and body are trained. Confusion that may conventionally be considered cultural can easily arise from such surreptitious causes, which may also prevent overt understanding from resolving an energetic unease.

In this connection it is useful to note that manipulation and perception of energy fields have multiple uses and values, which cannot be generalized for all situations. For example, a controlled release of energy can be used to convey a mood for decorous communication of feelings, or to draw a response to perceive another's mental state. Muting the energy field may be used for various purposes of stealth, health, or courtesy. Sensing another's field can likewise be an accomplice of aggression as well as of consideration. It is therefore a very deep and sensitive subject of concern in all human interaction, and naturally intensified in the context of conflict. The simplicity of Kansuke's expression is thus both elegant in its economy and effective in its acuity.

Two Assessments

Two assessments means assessing yourself and assessing adversaries.

Assessing yourself means understanding five advantages. The five advantages are the human advantage, the advantage of the ground, the advantage of the weather, the advantage of arms, and the advantage of assistance.

Next, assessing adversaries, means when to strike, and, after striking, noticing what's next.

If you assess yourself without assessing adversaries, or if you assess adversaries without assessing yourself, it will be hard to gain the advantage fairly.

Notes

The Chinese classic *The Art of War* by Sun Tzu, studied by all Japanese military scientists, speaks of strategic assessments in terms of comparing political leadership, military leadership, climate and terrain, troop strength, training, incentive, and discipline. Emphasizing the importance of these assessments, he writes, "If you know others and know yourself, you will not be imperiled in a hundred battles; if you do not know others but know yourself, you win one and lose one; if you do not know others and do not know yourself, you will be imperiled in every battle."[*]

---

[*] Cleary, *The Art of War,* p. 82.

Striking Enemies Unexpectedly

To strike an enemy unexpectedly, you should strike when it is evident in the enemy's body language and the look in his eyes, but he hasn't set his mind on his weapon yet. But even if the enemy has set his mind on his weapon, you can still strike before he draws his weapon from his scabbard.

Note

When it is evident means when you perceive there's going to be trouble. The idea is to discern the impulse before intent, in order to preempt an imminent attack.

The Frame of Mind on Missing a Stroke

In striking at an enemy, even as you try to strike when you feel the distance between you is right, you still may miss. This is called an empty strike. This is not only due to mistaking the distance between you; you can also miss because the enemy dodges or retreats. At such a time, you should consider it best to move right in, and dangerous to pull back.

Note

The point of moving right in is to crowd or tie up the adversary in order to blunt or confound a counterattack. An empty strike expends energy, and the momentum of a miss handicaps both recovery of poise and renewed attack. Under these conditions, pulling back would make one more vulnerable to counterattack, because the concrete conditions and configuration of the withdrawal are influenced by the posture and momentum of the miss, and to that extent the organic mechanism of perception and response is not optimally attuned to the action of the enemy in the critical moment after an empty strike.

Observing the Color and Expression of the Enemy's Face
In a fight or a duel, as you observe the enemy's face, if it reddens, that means he's excited. When you're excited, you don't plan how to win; your mind becomes hasty.

Next, when someone's face is pallid, that means fear. When the mind is fearful, you're reluctant to risk your life, so you only think of getting away, not discerning the decisive advantages that would enable you to strike enemies down.

Now then, to calculate advantage by observing an enemy's throat, you should recognize that when an adversary looks up he's figuring something at a distance, and when he looks down he is reckoning something nearby.

Discerning an Opponent's Strength or Weakness in His Voice
Discerning an opponent's strength or weakness by his voice refers to his voice when he's afraid, and his voice when he's strategically dissimulating. A fearful voice emerges from the kidneys; a dissimulating voice emerges from the heart.

There is also such a thing as progression and reversal of production and dying out of five sounds. Tradition says:

a	i	u	e	o
ka	*ki*	*ku*	*ke*	*ko*
spring	summer	earth	autumn	winter
sa	*shi*	*su*	*se*	*so*
liver	heart	spleen	lungs	kidneys
ta	*chi*	*tsu*	*te*	*to*
incisors	tongue	larynx	molars	lips
na	*ni*	*nu*	*ne*	*no*
blue	red	yellow	white	black
ha	*hi*	*fu*	*he*	*ho*
sweet	pungent	bitter	sour	salty
ma	*mi*	*mu*	*me*	*mo*
eyes	tongue	body	nose	ears
ya	*(y)i*	*yu*	*(y)e*	*yo*
east	south	center	west	north
ra	*ri*	*ru*	*re*	*ro*

wood produces fire produces earth produces metal
produces water

wa	*(w)i*	*u*	*(y)e*	*(w)o*

wood overcomes earth overcomes water overcomes
fire overcomes metal

In the progression and reversal of the production and
destruction of the five elements, there is an oral tradition
according to which there is reversal in progression, and
there is progression in reversal.

Notes

Voice analysis for detection of deception still captures considerable interest in a number of connections, both civil and military, but it is also extremely controversial in respect to the reliability of current methods. In Japanese, as in other languages, the same utterance can be made with different meanings, depending on the voice modulation. Formal speech is typically contrived for specific social and/or strategic purposes, and tone of voice is an important part of the art of representation.

An Opponent Who Does Not Act

An opponent who does not act means that even when weapons are drawn and you're on the verge of combat, there are opponents who do not withdraw yet do not advance, and don't even change their expression. You should not hasten to attack such an opponent without having any advantage. You should contrive to captivate him with your weapon. If his attention can't be captured, then you should retreat and strike only when you have an advantage.

Also, if an opponent gets captivated by weaponry technique, and his expression changes, it should be advantageous to strike.

Preemptive Victory, Preemptive Defeat

In military science there is preemptive victory and there is preemptive defeat. Preemptive victory means seeing advantage in striking early on and then striking successfully. Next, preemptive defeat means trying to strike an enemy first without having an advantage from which to strike, and thus getting struck by the enemy's counterattack.

Another example is when you strike first, but your weapon is dull and won't cut, so you get cut by your enemy's own weapon. Or you may strike a slight first blow and then get severely cut by the enemy's counter.

Two Against One

When there are two adversaries and you are dueling with them by yourself, take on both opponents head on. Make it seem like you're going for the one to your right, then go at the one on the left; as the opponent on your right backs up, step to the side and attack the opponent on your left.

Many Against One

When there are many opponents and you are alone, the advantage of the ground is foremost. If you cannot avail yourself of the advantage of the ground, strive to take on opponents on one front before you, fighting with the opponents to your left in the sunlight. As the opponents to your right are outside striking range, they'll probably circle around behind you. If they do circle, you should circle with them, sticking to the opponent on the extreme left. If you can't circle, and you are about to be surrounded, then you should run. The pursuit will be uneven, with some reaching you before others. Sidestep and strike the first to come. Those who come running at you won't be able to stop, making it possible to strike them as they go by.

A Contest Between One Opponent and a Group of Allies
If your opponent is one individual, and you have an ally, you and your ally should attack from front and back. If you are three, attack from three sides. If you are four, attack from four sides. If you are ten, there is a technique of attacking him from ten sides.

Notes
The term *ri* for *advantage* also means *technique.* Attack from ten sides requires a certain protocol to be effective, for ten allies rushing on one opponent at once would inhibit and injure each other with their weapons, and enable the opponent to inflict more damage before succumbing.

Striking an Onrush
To strike someone who rushes at you, he cannot be hit head on, so it is advantageous to let him rush past you and strike the adversary from behind him to his right.

Note
This means turning the momentum of the adversary's onslaught against him to your own advantage by sidestepping it rather than meeting it head on.

Chasing Those Who Run
When it comes to chasing those who run, up to ten paces you should keep after them like the wind to strike them. Further than that, however, pursuit must be careful, for an

enemy may sidestep and try to strike you, or an enemy may drop down to try to strike you.

First, if someone tries to sidestep to strike you, pull up short and stop as soon as you see a sign he's going to do that; get the enemy to draw his weapon first, and strike him with a follow-up counter blow. If you can't stop yourself as you're running, go past the enemy's right rear and strike.

Next, if he drops down to try to strike you, either dodge to the side or pull back; getting the enemy to draw his sword first, you have the advantage in striking with a follow-up counter blow.

Striking Someone Who Has Taken Cover

To strike someone who's taken cover, first make sure to see whether it's a samurai or a servant. If it's a samurai, you should strike immediately, while if it's a servant you should wait a while to strike.

The reason for this is that in the case of a samurai, once he's acted cowardly, he has no way to go on living even if he escapes on that occasion. Therefore, if he has time, he'll contrive to leave his reputation intact. Then in the case of a servant, if he has time he'll want to live, so he'll gradually become more timid.

Striking Someone Who Is Down

To strike someone who's down, if he's lying face up, strike from the direction of his head. If you can't approach from the direction of his head, strike him from his left side. If you can't approach on the left either, be cautious about going

around to his right side. A prostrate enemy's sword to protect his right comes out sweep-slashing, so your advantage
is in striking with a follow-up counter blow after deflecting
the enemy's slash.

When an Enemy Comes upon You from Behind

When an enemy comes upon on you from behind, says
something to you and tries to strike you, your advantage is
in sidestepping to the right.

Note

The sidestep pivots on the right foot, out of the trajectory
of the enemy's assault, blending the momentum of the
pivot into a counterattack.

Fighting a Mounted Opponent on Foot

When you fight an enemy who is on horseback while you
are on foot, your advantage is in sweep-slashing the horse's
legs first, then striking the enemy when he falls.

Notes

The author of this text was an infantry soldier and commander; these instructions are for foot soldiers. Horsemen
naturally have different perceptions of horses due to their
habitual symbiotic relationship in combat. When horsemen are thrown off horseback in combat, or are attacked
before they can mount, unlike infantry soldiers they are
not expected to slash a horse before the rider. Horsemen
would be expected to be more viscerally reluctant to kill a

horse than a man, because of having been specially trained to ride horses and to kill men; therefore, in a situation facing a mounted enemy while on foot themselves, and where the object is to kill men, not horses, people trained as horsemen would be more effective aiming to slashing the rider's legs rather than the horse's legs.

Fighting in a Crowd

When you fight in the midst of a crowd, move so that you won't have the people behind you. If anyone is behind you, you can be caught off guard.

Winning and Losing in a Mutual Strike

Victory in a mutual strike means:

- Your hand may get cut, but you cut off the enemy's head.
- You may suffer a superficial wound but you inflict a deep wound on the enemy.
- Your left hand may get cut, but you cut off the enemy's left leg.

All other examples are analogous to these three.

PART IX

Advantages of Terrain

Fighting with Space Between You and the Enemy
In a contest where there is space between the enemy and you, wait for the enemy to come; don't go yourself. There are tremendous advantages in waiting. First is the advantage of not taxing your body. Second is the advantage of your mind being undisturbed. Third is the advantage of having time to contrive your preparation. Fourth is the advantage of not getting stuck in a bad spot. Fifth is the advantage of naturally being able to take advantage of the weather.

Even so, if your location is bad, note in front, behind, left, and right, and find advantageous ground to await the enemy.

Fighting an Enemy Coming from Afar
When fighting an enemy who's come from afar, you should attack them to take away their spirit. The logic of this is that

those who have come from afar are mentally fatigued and physically exhausted, so they're handicapped in action. Even so, a prudent enemy will stay unmoving to figure out how to win, so the advantage of taking away their spirit and heart is paramount.

So the body is drawn by mind, the mind is drawn by spirit. When the mood is affected, the mind is affected; and when the mind is affected, the body is affected. Do not dare to take this principle lightly.

Notes

As before, in this usage *spirit* has no association with spirituality but means "spunk." The original character, which here refers to the vigor of the so-called fighting spirit, includes meanings of mood and energy. Manipulation of mood to influence mental and physical energy in quantity, quality, and orientation, is an active element of psychological operations as well as material warfare.

Fighting on a Slope

In a contest on a slope, it is advantageous to be on higher ground. First is the advantage of looking down on the enemy. Second is the advantage of ease in advancing on the enemy. Third is the advantage of having no danger above you.

Nevertheless, even if you're on higher ground, if the footing is bad you should get out of that spot.

In getting out, there are three guidelines to understand.

First, to go to higher ground behind you, keep calm and don't step too high.

Second, to dodge to the left or right, be actively alert and step lightly.

Third, to go to lower ground, you should run like the wind. If the enemy pursues you, your advantage is in sidestepping to strike. That advantage is the fact that the momentum of running downhill can't be halted at will, so he'll go right by; therefore it's advantageous for you to pivot out of the way and strike the enemy. The same advantage can be used when an enemy is on higher ground and you are on lower ground.

Fighting on a Narrow Path

A narrow path means both sides are impassable, with no way through; a pathway that is straight and narrow. On such terrain, when you are alone against many opponents, you can take advantage of it. The advantage is that even though there are many opponents they cannot encircle you. And if opponents come from in front and behind, pivot to the side and face them, engaging the opponent to your left.

Also it is traditionally said that if there is a shallow river or a shallow pond beside the path, it is also advantageous to jump in. To get the advantage, you have to jump in first; when the opponent jumps in after you, this is when you have got your poise while the opponent has lost his poise. Thus you have the advantage to strike him.

Fighting Where the Way is Cut Off

A fight where the way is cut off means there is no way to the left, right, or rear, while in front there are many opponents.

In such a situation, you should give no thought to escape; taking death for granted, you should figure how best to leave a good reputation.

Another tradition says that in cases where there is a river on both sides, or ponds, or deep fields, and there is a steep mountain behind, you should reckon advantage without fleeing or retreating.

Also, where there are mountains on either side and a pond behind, first climb a mountain to an advantageous spot to fight.

Fighting on an Open Road

In a fight on an open road, when you have few opponents and many allies, it is advantageous to encircle them and strike.

Then again, when you are alone against numerous opponents, you should maneuver so that you are facing them all. But as the adversaries are so numerous, they attack from both sides; then, feinting engagement with opponents on your right, engage the opponents on your left; feinting engagement with opponents on your left, engage the opponents on your right.

Maneuvering this way, ultimately you should circle, sticking to opponents to the left. But being so numerous, the enemy tries to surround you. Then you should run. Even if the enemy pursues you en masse, they won't reach you all at once; so there is advantage in sidestepping and striking the first to come, or dropping to strike. This technique is also noted in the scroll on human advantage.

Using the Terrain to Your Right When You Fight

Things like mountains, rivers, cliffs, levees, doors, walls, or screens should be to your right when you fight. Always keeping advantages to your right is a traditional teaching.

And don't forget that what is advantageous to you, the enemy may occupy.

Terrain You Should Not Have Behind You When You Fight

Mountains, rivers, ponds, marshes, flooded fields, rocky ground, sandy terrain, grassy meadows, or downhill ground should not be behind you. You cannot maneuver forward and back freely, so you'll get caught off guard.

Then again, if you do have your back to an impasse, pivot so your left side is forward; that way you can naturally make use of the impasse to your right side.

Fighting on Stone Stairs

When fighting on stone stairs, if you're near level ground, move to the level ground while keeping your enemy on the stairs to fight.

If both you and the enemy are far from level ground, fighting in the middle of the stairs, if they are gently sloping stairs keep the enemy below and stay above; if they are steep stairs, keep the enemy above and stay below.

It is also said that on a stone staircase it is feasible to maneuver sideways.

Fighting Storming a Castle

To fight while storming a castle, keep a wall on your right. If you're in the middle of people, you cannot maneuver freely. In particular, first of all there is the advantage of ease in moving forward; second there is the advantage of being able to use your weapons freely; third is the advantage of warding off enemy arrows; fourth is the advantage of certainty of success.

Striking in the Country and Striking in Town

In the countryside, first cut off your enemy's leg; in town, make it your priority to cut off your enemy's head.

The reason for this is that in the country one cannot fight with a leg cut off; even if he screams, being far from human habitations there is no one to come to his aid. This is to your advantage.

Now then, in a town, to cut off his head is advantageous in that you don't let him call for help.

Some say that one can survive having a leg cut off, but there is no life once the head is severed, so you should cut off the head whether in the country or in a town. The answer to this is that the legs are long and thus easy to cut, while the neck is short and it is possible to fail to cut it; so whether in the country on in a town, if people are far away you should cut a leg first, while if people are nearby you should cut off the head.

Notes

Some range of degree could be construed in the interpretation of the verb for *cutting*, but in the context of sword fighting the implication is usually severing. In the case of the head, though it is comparatively easy to inflict a fatal blow with a sword by severing an artery, it was an ancient custom in China as well as Japan to sever heads for body count and reckoning of rewards. In targeting legs to disable an adversary, depending on position it may be possible to sever an artery, cut a tendon, or amputate the limb with the low sweep-slash.

Fighting Across a Gate or Door

In a fight across a doorway, there is an advantage when you are one against many. The advantage is that even though there are many opponents, they cannot encircle you to strike. However, if they have time, enemies may come around by another way, so you should keep yourself covered.

Fighting an Enemy on the Other Side of a Door or Screen

When you know there's an enemy on the other side of a door or screen, and you are about to fight, if the enemy is on your left, you should recognize that an adversary with his sword overhead is intending to cut you, while you should figure that an adversary with his sword pointed in front of him is intending to stab you, and so you come out with your sword forward low and even.

If the enemy is on your right, if his sword is in a middle position he's intending to sweep-slash, while if it's overhead, figure he's going to strike, and so come out with your body low and your sword low and down.

It is also traditionally said, "Don't oppose the formless."

Note
The last admonition means that it is critical to know the enemy's disposition before engaging.

Fighting Inside a House
To engage in a battle inside a house, first calculate the length and width of the room. Next, figure out where it is advantageous and where there are obstacles; stay where it is advantageous, and put your opponent in a difficult spot.

Also, if it's in your own house, you should delay; if it's in another's house, you should contrive to prevail right away.

Notes
The reason for recommending delay in one's own house is that one is intimately familiar with the layout and thus already knows the most advantageous places to take a stand and the most advantageous places to trap an opponent, so it is worthwhile taking the time to maneuver precisely, thus minimizing exposure to counterattack and destruction of one's home in the process. In another's house, one is unfamiliar with the layout and also does not know who else might be there or could show up, so it is advantageous to settle a contest as quickly as possible, before being maneuvered into an

unforeseen impasse, or set upon by another member or associate of the house suddenly coming upon the confrontation.

Fighting in the Bush
In the bush means in places like woods and groves. In such places you can get advantage using short weapons. Don't use anything like a hooked spear or cross-head spear.

Note
In the thicket of natural obstructions of the bush, weapons like a hooked spear or a cross-head spear would be difficult to wield freely and would easily get stuck, making it impossible to sweep, thrust, or retract and recover reliably.

Fighting on Ground Where the Footing is Bad
When fighting on ground where the footing is bad, you should figure out how to get the advantage without moving your body. If, however, the footing is bad ahead but there's good footing behind, first stand where the footing is bad, then at the appropriate moment retreat to where there's good footing, putting the enemy where the footing is bad.

Fighting in a River
In a fight standing in a river, keep your adversary upstream, while you face him diagonally downstream to his right.

The reasons for this are, first, the principle of taking on positive energy when you face the current; and second, so as not to be troubled by flotsam coming from upriver.

Notes

Taking on positive energy when you face the current is based on the fundamental principle of "awaiting the enemy." By keeping the enemy upriver you are in a position to take advantage of the momentum of the current as it impels the enemy toward you. In theory, the enemy can use this momentum too, but it compromises his control and works against him if he misses, as the swivel sidestep and strike counter used when fleeing downhill can also be used here.

Fighting on a Makeshift Bridge

A makeshift bridge is a rickety bridge. When fighting there, you should get off the bridge to induce your opponent onto the bridge to fight. That is because one cannot maneuver freely on a rickety bridge.

If you can't get off, then you should contrive to get your opponent onto the bridge too.

Also, if you are on a rickety bridge when enemies come at you from front and back, you can get the advantage by jumping into the river.

Note

The advantage of jumping into the river, beyond getting out of the immediate pickle, is the advantage of being the first to jump in if adversaries follow, as explained earlier in the text, giving oneself time to get set and go on the offensive while putting the adversary in temporary disarray.

Fighting in Boats

In a fight in boats at a bend, if they're far off shoot their boats with guns. If they're close, use something like a cross-head spear, "bear paw," or fire axe hook to pull the boat near, make it list, and strike the enemy.

Note

A *bear paw* was a weapon used to hook an opponent's neck. The same word in civilian usage means "rake."

Fighting on Landing

In a fight upon landing, get onto shore first, while your adversary is still in the boat, and strike him as he tries to climb out.

If you have no way to climb onshore, retreat and continue to keep your opponent in the boat too.

Notes

The text is ambiguous as to whether it is referring specifically to one or two boats, but the principle is the same in either case. If the adversaries are both in the same boat, the premise is that they have waited to land in order to fight because the instability of a boat on water makes for poor footing and bad balance, and limitations of form and dimension restrict maneuvers. If the adversaries are in different boats, they may wait to land to fight because the equipment or conditions for successfully shooting or capsizing the enemy, as recommended in the preceding segment, happen to be unavailable. In either case, the aim to is gain stable ground before the opponent, then attack while the opponent is still unstable.

PART X

Advantages of the Sky

Moods of the Five Seasons
Human beings, born between sky and earth, inherit their patterns. For this reason it is a natural pattern to be active in spring, vigorous in summer, quiet in autumn, and withdrawn in winter. Using this to figure out your state of mind and that of your enemy, in spring and summer the mind, drawn by yang energy, becomes very bold, but is also easily discouraged.

> *Don't meet enemies racing toward you head-on;*
> *Maneuver to make them miss their timing.*

Anyway, in fall and winter the mind quiets down somberly. Though not daring, it still has courage, so it is considered best to strike as soon as you apprehend the pattern.

Notes

The last admonition means that even if an adversary is sluggish and disinclined to fight, there is still underlying character, which given time can mobilize; so the strategy is to attack an enemy in this state before he has a chance to awaken his courage. On the physical level, it also means to strike adversaries when they're stiff, before they limber up, as "cold" muscles act more slowly and have less capacity to disperse or absorb the energy of a blow, or to dodge an assault and deliver a counter attack.

Fighting in the Sun

When you fight in the sun, keep the sun to your back. There is the advantage of becoming energized, and also when you get your opponent to face the sun his eyes will be dazzled and he won't be able to see your look.

Note

If the adversary can't see your look, he can't read your eye movements or facial expression to anticipate your actions.

Fighting in Moonlight

When fighting on a moonlit night, keep in the dark while getting your opponent to face the moon. The advantage in this is that you remain hidden while exposing the adversary to view.

Notes

Remaining hidden while exposing the other is a general principle of strategy that is also applied in traditional Chinese political science. The design is that rulers keep their own thoughts unknown to thwart opportunistic sycophants by making it impossible for them to be sure how to curry favor, causing them to expose themselves in the course of their attempts to do so. *The Master of Demon Valley* says, "You need to be equanimous and calm yourself to listen to people's statements, examine their affairs, assess myriad things, and distinguish relative merits.... When you have thoroughly clarified matters yourself, and have determined measures whereby it is possible to govern others, and yet you reveal no obvious form, so that no one can see into your privacy, this is called genius."*

Fighting on a Dark Night

When fighting on a dark night, keep low; descry the enemy's silhouette, and figure out what form of weaponry he's wielding. If there are any obstacles, keep them in front of you as you fight.

Note

Figuring out what form of weaponry the adversary is wielding implies calculating the characteristic movements to expect, the range of the weapon and the margin of safety, the placement of the adversary's hands and feet, the

---

* Cleary, *Thunder in the Sky,* pp. 12, 13.

configurations of advantageous avoidance maneuvers and counter attacks, and the places where employment of that weapon will be hampered by features of the surroundings.

Fighting in the Wind

Wind blows differently in the four seasons. First, the spring wind blows from earth to sky. Summer wind blows level. Autumn wind blows down from above. Winter wind blows downward.

With this understanding, maneuver so as to have the wind at your back. When you have the wind at your back, you're not impeded by the wind, and it helps you move forward. There is also another reason: this has the advantage that when you get your adversary to face the wind, his eyes will blur, and he won't see ahead of him, only a sense of attention being drawn backward.

In a high wind, there is advantage in facing the wind.

Note

The advantage of facing a high wind is in exploiting the adversary's momentum as he is propelled toward you, such as by the swiveling sidestep maneuver to dodge the onslaught and strike the enemy as his momentum carries him past you.

Fighting Indoors on a Windy Night

A fight inside a house differs depending on whether it's your own house or someone else's house. If you go into another's house to fight, keep the walls to your back, or to your right. Doors and screens are useless at your back, and, what is more, in the wind they rattle and you might be startled.

Notes
Keeping the walls to one's back or right in another's house is to avoid being surrounded or outflanked, and to keep continuous track of accessible, defendable, and maneuverable space. Doors and screens are useless at your back because they can be opened or broken through. The rattling of a door or screen would sound like others entering the room, naturally distracting the attention from the adversary at hand.

Fighting in the Rain
When fighting in the rain, keeping outside striking distance, lower your head and watch the form of the enemy's weapon. Wielding your sword in an upper position you can get the advantage.

Notes
One advantage of an upper sword position in the rain is that if the adversary looks up the rain will blur his vision, so it is harder for him to observe the disposition of your sword. Another advantage is that of maximum force on a sword stroke while on slippery ground, with the predominance of arm and torso effort minimizing the need for

drive through the legs from the feet. Sideways or upwards strokes from middle or lower positions would increase the chances of the feet slipping and dissipating or disrupting the force of the body's drive on the sword.

Fighting in the Snow

When fighting in the snow, if snow has accumulated on the ground, wait at a safe distance for the enemy to come— don't go to him. If it isn't accumulating on the ground and not much snow is falling, wield your weapon in an upper position and contrive to get the enemy to look upward.

Notes

Waiting in accumulated snow is for saving energy, preserving an advantageous position, and keeping a sound footing. If snow isn't accumulating on the ground, then it cannot be used to slow and tire an enemy or get him to slip as he attacks; but as long as some snow is falling, it can be used to blur his vision if he can be induced to look upward by wielding your weapon in an upper position.

Fighting in the Cold

When fighting on a cold day or a cold night, your hands and feet go numb and you can't feel your grip on your weapon, and might even drop it. For this reason, it's good to keep some raw ginger in your mouth, and rub your hand and feet with *sake.*

Fighting an Enemy from Afar in the Cold

When fighting an enemy who's come from afar on a cold day or a cold night, you have the natural advantage. Nevertheless, because of the tradition that one should neither despise the weak nor fear the strong, it is most proper to calculate advantages on top of this advantage.

Fighting in a Thunderstorm

When fighting while thunder is booming, if you master the pattern it becomes your ally, whereas if you err it becomes your enemy. The reasoning behind this is the pattern of being startled or not being startled.

Even if you're startled, it will thunder when it thunders and won't when it doesn't; and the same is so even if you're not startled, so why be startled? Just make the thunder your ally and strike the enemy when he's startled.

Notes

"Why be startled" means that the thunder is independent of the reaction, so the reaction (or non-reaction) should be independent of the thunder. There is nothing that can be done about the thunder but to detach the attention. This detachment, an essential element of defense under these conditions, can be fostered by intensified focus on the disposition of the enemy, an essential element of offense, in order take advantage of a moment of distraction on the part of the adversary.

Fighting in a Lightning Storm

When fighting in a lightning storm, keep its light to your back, getting the enemy to be facing the light. This is because first, it shows his form; second, it obstructs his vision; third, it takes away his spunk; fourth, it distracts his mind.

Not Choosing Auspicious Dates

In the arts of warfare, let the enemy be influenced by the choice of date; don't take much stock in it yourself. A song says,

> *A bad day*
> *Is not different for enemies and allies;*
> *All that is essential*
> *Is ingenuity and training.*

Even in people who are said to be experts in the whole science, if their mentality is ignorant, these superstitions prevail. Reading a chessboard, modeled on warfare, even if you're in an unfavorable position winning is a matter of skill.

Due to confusion,
The triple world is walled;
By virtue of enlightenment,
The ten directions are empty.
Originally there is no east or west;
Where could south or north be?

—Yamamoto Kansuke

Notes

The triple world, a Buddhist term, refers to the domains of desire, form, and formless phenomena such as consciousness and space. The point of this verse is that fixed systems cannot capture the texture of experience mechanically with enough sophistication and subtlety to analyze and predict reliably. This is one meaning of the Taoist dictum, "A way that can be spoken is not a permanent way." In the science of strategy this principle is embodied in repeated emphasis on adaptation and change. By the same token, the strategic value of encouraging superstitions in adversaries is precisely to make them less adaptable and more predictable, thus more vulnerable. This combination of denial and exploitation of superstitious systems is referred to as being formless yourself while trapping the enemy in a form.